FLOWER HERDING
ON MOUNT MONADNOCK

BY GALWAY KINNELL:

WHAT A KINGDOM IT WAS

FLOWER HERDING ON MOUNT MONADNOCK

FLOWER HERDING

ON MOUNT MONADNOCK

BY GALWAY KINNELL

1964

HOUGHTON MIFFLIN COMPANY BOSTON

THE RIVERSIDE PRESS CAMBRIDGE

300

Certain of the poems in this volume have previously appeared in various
books and magazines as follows:

The Beloit Poetry Journal: "Tillamook Journal (2nd version)." Copyright
© 1963 by Galway Kinnell.

Chelsea: "Old Arrivals." Copyright © 1960 by Galway Kinnell.

Choice: "For Denise Levertov." Copyright © 1961 by Galway Kinnell.

The Hudson Review: "River That Is East," "Calcutta Visits," "To a Child
in Calcutta," "Flower Herding on Mount Monadnock." Copyright © 1961
by Galway Kinnell. "Room of Return," "On Hardscrabble Mountain,"
"A Bird Comes Back," "Poem of Night." Copyright © 1964 by Galway
Kinnell.

The Paris Review: "On Frozen Fields," "Last Spring."

Poetry: "The Homecoming of Emma Lazarus." Copyright © 1961 by
Galway Kinnell. "Ruins under the Stars." Copyright © 1964 by The
Modern Poetry Association.

The Princeton University Library Chronicle: "Nightfall of the Real."
Copyright © 1964 by Galway Kinnell.

The Nation: "Koisimi Buddhist of Altitudes," "Hunger unto Death"
(under the title "Lunch Hour"), "Cells Breathe in the Emptiness."
Copyright © 1961, 1963, by Galway Kinnell.

CONTENTS

PART I

THE RIVER THAT IS EAST

1

Buoys begin clanging like churches
And peter out. Sunk to the gunwhales
In their shapes tugs push upstream.
A carfloat booms down, sweeping past
Illusory suns that blaze in puddles
On the shores where it rained, past the Navy Yard,
Under the Williamsburg Bridge
That hangs facedown from its strings
Over which the Jamaica Local crawls,
Through white-winged gulls which shriek
And flap from the water and sideslip in
Over the chaos of illusions, dangling
Limp red hands, and screaming as they touch.

2

A boy swings his legs from the pier,
His days go by, tugs and carfloats go by,
Each prow pushing a whitecap. On his deathbed
Kane remembered the abrupt, missed Grail
Called Rosebud, Gatsby must have thought back
On his days digging clams in Little Girl Bay
In Minnesota, Nick fished in dreamy Michigan,
Gant had his memories, Griffeths, those
Who went baying after the immaterial
And whiffed its strange dazzle in a blonde
In a canary convertible, who died

3

Thinking of the Huck Finns of themselves
On the old afternoons, themselves like this boy
Swinging his legs, who sees the *Ile de France*
Come in, and wonders if in some stateroom
There is not a sick-hearted heiress sitting
Drink in hand, saying to herself his name.

3

A man stands on the pier.
He has long since stopped wishing his heart were full
Or his life dear to him.
He watches the snowfall hitting the dirty water.
He thinks: Beautiful. Beautiful.
If I were a gull I would be one with white wings,
I would fly out over the water, explode, and
Be beautiful snow hitting the dirty water.

4

And thou, River of Tomorrow, flowing . . .
We stand on the shore, which is mist beneath us,
And regard the onflowing river. Sometimes
It seems the river stops and the shore
Flows into the past. Nevertheless, its leaked promises
Hopping in the bloodstream, we strain for the future,
Sometimes even glimpse it, a vague, scummed thing
We dare not recognize, and peer again
At the cabled shroud out of which it came,
We who have no roots but the shifts of our pain,
No flowering but our own strange lives.

What is this river but the one
Which drags the things we love,
Processions of debris like floating lamps,
Towards the radiance in which they go out?

No, it is the River that is East, known once
From a high window in Brooklyn, in agony — river
On which a door locked to the water floats,
A window sash paned with brown water, a whisky crate,
Barrel staves, sun spokes, feathers of the birds,
A breadcrust, a rat, spittle, butts, and peels,
The immaculate stream, heavy, and swinging home again.

THE HOMECOMING OF EMMA LAZARUS

1

Having no father anymore, having got up
In England without hope, having sailed the strewn
Atlantic and been driven under Bedloe
In the night, where the Green Lady lifts
Over that slow, bleating, most tragic of harbors,

Her burning hand, Emma came floating home,
To the thick, empty whistling of the tugs.
Thoreau's pocket compass had been her keepsake,
She made her way in without it, through the fog,
It was hard for her, in fact, coming in to die,

A little unfair, her father having died already.
In the attic on Union Square? Thrown out? Ah,
Somewhere in the mess of things! From Governor's Island
A bugler's loneliest notes roll slowly in,
And birds rock in the fog on the slapping waves.

2

As a child she had chased a butterfly
Through Battery Park, the only one decorating
Manhattan that afternoon, its clumsy, wind-thin
Wings making cathedral windows in the sun,

While the despised grandmother
With the gleety leashes, cruddy with age,
Of the eyebeams, held on. Alas, the crone's
Doughy ears must also have been golden in the sun!

It was towards you, gilded in the day's going down,
Green Lady, that we crawled — but from what ground of
    nausea
Had we turned, what relinquished plot of earth
Had we spit at, which was, anyway, the earth?

3

Dark haired, ephebic Emma, you knew
The night you floated into New York Harbor
Atlantis had sunk while you were abroad,
You could see the rainbows of it shining queerly
The many thousand leagues of your life away —

Weekends on Union Square, from his shaving mug
You blew bubbles crawling with colors that buoyed
Into the sunshine, you made up little rhymes,
You skipped rope, at your father's knee he put
Lilacs in your hair. Everybody loved you!

And on the last ride across 14th,
Did the English success suddenly become nothing,
Did the American childhood, including the odd affliction,
Your neurotic longing to be English, turn out
To be the one paradise you died longing for?

4

Facing the Old World the Green Lady whispers, "Eden!"
Seeing her looking so trim in American verdigris
They thought she was saying how it was here,
Seeing her looking to sea we heard the pure nostalgia,
Vacuumed in the wind from the Dry Cleaning Store
She may, herself, have wondered what she meant.

She crouches on the floor. She read once,
In the paper, a poem she had composed herself.

Was it just poetry, all that? It was pretty,
There is nothing she can do about it, it really was.
Her arm lies along the bench, her hand
Hangs over the edge as if she has just let something drop.

She has wept a long time now, and now poetry
Can do no more to her. Her shoulder shrugs as though
To drive away birds which, anyway, weren't intending
To alight. In the Harbor the conscript bugler
Blows the old vow of acceptance into the night —
It fades, and the wounds of all we had accepted open.

OLD ARRIVALS

Molded in verdigris
Shortly before she died
The Lady stands by herself
Her electrical hand on fire.

They too in the Harbor
That chops the light to pieces
Looked up at her hand, burning,
Hair, flesh, blood, bone.

They floated in at night
On black water, cargoes
Which may not go back, waves
Breaking the rocks they break on.

HUNGER UNTO DEATH

Her underarms
Clean as washbasins,
Her folds of fat resting
On layers of talcum-powdered flesh,
She proceeds towards cream-cheese-on-white,
Jelly pie, gum brownies, chocolate bars,
Rinsed down by tumblers of fresh milk,

Past the Trinity Graveyard
Filled with green, creepy plants,
Shiny-necked birds waddling about,
Monuments three-humped like children playing ghost,
Blackstone slabs racked with dates and elegies,

At which,
In the dark of the wide skirt,
First left then right,
Like a political campaigner pulling out of a station,
Her heavy rear rolls out its half-smiles of farewell,

While the face wheezes for grub,
And sweat skips and splashes from hummock down to
    hummock,
And inconceivable love clasps the fat of life to its pain.

CALCUTTA VISITS

Overhead the fan wobbles on its axle.
In Delhi, on Gandhi's tomb, it said *Hai Ram* ("an old cry").
On Sudden Street they cry, "Hey Johnny,
Nice girl? Chinese, Indian, European, Mixed?"
She taps a fat foot, finicks with phonograph needles,
Fools with buttons. "No like dance,"
She announces, collapsing on the carpet, "Fookey!"
The bird will leave this branch at dawn
And fly away. For one full day remember her.

From this blue window? this blue, zigzagging street?
(*"Five? Five* already? Ah, den come morning . . .")
A man in white skids towards your knees,
"A morsel! A morsel!" The only city
In the world where the beggars have read Dickens,
Says the Oxford Indian of his first homecoming,
As he sits up there in the Grand Hotel,
Among bribed, sleepy bellhops, drinking himself blind,
While the fan prowls the ceiling as in a zoo.

Floodtime. Cabs practically floating through town.
The driver sizes me up in the rearview mirror
With black, mystical eyes: how exactly to soak me . . .
A Bengal poet, disciple of Tagore,
His tongue flickering through his talk like a serpent's,
Looks from his window on the city. He says
Each day he has to transcend its pain anew.
His face darkens by the window and gives nothing away.
It is his pain, by the love that asks no way out.

DOPPELGÄNGER

1

I have to bribe the policeman
To keep him from arresting the driver
For trying to make me overpay him, which I've just done.

A sailor staggers up,
All his money blown on thieves he cries,
I pay him and he goes off hunting more thieves.

The fan whips up the heat,
The ice turns to slush
Before you can throw it in your whisky.

2

I remember at daybreak,
The air on the point of cooling
Was just starting to heat up,

I heard a voice in the distance,
I looked up, far away,
There at the beginning of the world

I could make out a beggar,
Down the long street he was calling *Galway!*
I started towards him and began calling *Galway!*

TO A CHILD IN CALCUTTA

Dark child in my arms, eyes
The whites of them just like mine
Gazing with black, shined canniness
At mine like large agates in a billboard,

Whom I held as a passerby
A few stricken days down Bandook Gulli,
While they were singing, upstairs,
Everyone in Calcutta is knocking at my door,

You are my conqueror! and you were
Calmly taking in my colored eyes and
Skin burned and thin and
Browned hardly at all by your Bengal sun:

If they show you, when you reach my age,
The blown-up snapshot they took of the stranger
Holding all you once were in his arms,
What will you be able to think, then,

Of the one who came from some elsewhere
And took you in his arms
And let you know the touch of a father
And the old warmth in a paw from nowhere,

But that in his nowhere
He will be dying, letting go his hold
On all for which his heart tore itself
As when they snapped you in his arms like his child,

And going by the photograph
That there was this man, his hair in his eyes,
His hand bigger than your whole head,
Who held you when helplessly

You let him, that between him and you
Were this gesture and this allowance
And he is your stranger father
And he dies in a strange land, which is his own.

In Calcutta, I thought,
Every pimp, taxidriver, whore, and beggar,
Dowsed for me through the alleys day and night —
In Bandook Gulli I came upon you,

On a street crossed by fading songs
I held you in my arms
Until you slept, in these arms,
In rags, in the pain of a little flesh.

KYOTO PRINTS

for Makoto, Koisimi and Miss Mori

1

In the green air
Of before the dawn
The gutterals of the prayer
Pile up on formal hiccups.

2

The lake
Every point on whose shore
Keeps out of sight of some other point
Is drawn from the kokorai,
A character drawn from the heart.
In it is a flaw called the Pure Land.

3

A phallic,
Thousand-year gravestone rises,
Miko pick their way past
With chalk faces, on big shoes,
Pucka pucka pucka pucka

4

After the Ceremony of Kō
The girl draws out the coals
And pokes nine vents in the clay
To let out the old fire smell.

5

Tied to a few leaves
Attached loosely to the air
In the garden of moss and pine
An old eye with a spider in it
No longer troubles to look out,
A common disease of the eye
(With a pretty name:
I-Saw-the-Ghost-of-a-Flower . . .)

KOISIMI BUDDHIST OF ALTITUDES

He sees a skinny waterfall hanging
Like a bare root, a shape seeking water
Down which the particles of water crawl,
And climbs, crawling up the shined
Rock rubbing his fingerprints off,
And looks from the top at the land,
As it was, clawed from within, perfectly
Unbroken. He cries, *it is me,*
At the glare, and waits, and he hears
On the horizon the thin whine of wind
Machining its way to where he waits.
The first eddies begin picking up speed,
Sunlight and rock start circling
Around him, now they lose hold, and skid
Some degrees, appear to recover,
And now skid all the way out, and vanish.
What is this wind? Koisimi challenges.
It is not me, he knows, and leans
In any direction, which is the way.

LAST SPRING

1

Through a dark winter
In a cold chambre de bonne
I lay still and dreamt

And as we lose our grip
On every real thing in the world
Settling for its glitter

It was of the things
Whose corpses eclipse them,
Shellfishes, ostriches, elephants.

2

But in spring the sun's
Swath of reality started going over
The room daily, like a cleaning woman,

It sent up my keepsakes,
My inventions in dust,
It left me only a life

And time to walk
Head bobbing out front like a pigeon's
Knocking on the instants to let me in.

ROOM OF RETURN

Room over the Hudson
Where a naked light bulb
Lights coat hangers, whisky bottles,
Umbrellas, anti-war tracts, poems,
A potted plant trimmed to a crucifixion,

From which, out the front window,
You sometimes see
The *Vulcania* or the *France*
Or a fat *Queen*
Steaming through the buildings across the street,

To which every night
The alleycat sneaks up
To slop his saucer
Of fresh milk on the fire escape,
Washing down his rat,

Room crossed by winds from
Air conditioners' back ends,
By the clicking at all hours of invisible looms,
By cries of the night-market, hoofbeats, horns,
By bleats of boats lost on the Hudson,

Room, anyway,
Where I switch the light on
After an absence of years
Tiny glimmer again in this city
Pricking the sky, shelled by the dirty sea.

FOR DENISE LEVERTOV

Denise when you recited
With your intense unmusical voice
Poems on the objects of faith,
Buildings, rocks, birds, oranges,
A bum stood outside on Bleecker
Looking in through the glass
At you sitting in your green robe
Amid the Old World longhand
Of your utter, gently uttered
Solitude. Had you glanced up,
And had you seen his liquored eye,
The mowed cornfield of his gawk,
Maybe suddenly you would have seen
Him eye to eye, and paused,
And then gone on, in a room
Of cigarette smoke and coffee smells
And faithful friends, the hapless
Witness crying again in your breast.

UNDER THE WILLIAMSBURG BRIDGE

1

I broke bread
At the riverbank,
I saw the black gull
Fly back black and crossed
By the decaying Paragon sign in Queens,
Over ripped water, it screamed
Killing the ceremony of the dove,
I cried those wing muscles
Tearing for life at my bones.

2

Tomorrow,
There on the Bridge,
Up in some riveted cranny in the sky,
It is true, the great and wondrous sun will be shining
On an old spider wrapping a fly in spittle-strings.

FOR ROBERT FROST

1

Why do you talk so much
Robert Frost? One day
I drove up to Ripton to ask,

I stayed the whole day
And never got the chance
To put the question.

I drove off at dusk
Worn out and aching
In both ears. Robert Frost,

Were you shy as a boy?
Do you go on making up
For some long stint of solitude?

Is it simply that talk
Doesn't have to be metered and rhymed?
Or is gab distracting from something worse?

2

I saw you once on the TV,
Unsteady at the lectern,
The flimsy white leaf
Of hair standing straight up
In the wind, among top hats,
Old farmer and son

Of worse winters than this,
Stopped in the first dazzle

Of the District of Columbia,
Suddenly having to pay
For the cheap onionskin,
The worn-out ribbon, the eyes
Wrecked from writing poems
For us — stopped,
Lonely before millions,
The paper jumping in your grip,

And as the Presidents
Also on the platform
Began flashing nervously
Their Presidential smiles
For the harmless old guy,
And poets watching on the TV
Started thinking, Well that's
The end of *that* tradition,

And the managers of the event
Said, Boys this is it,
This sonofabitch poet
Is gonna croak,
Putting the paper aside
You drew forth
From your great faithful heart
The poem.

3

Once, walking in winter in Vermont,
In the snow, I followed a set of footprints
That aimed for the woods. At the verge
I could make out, "far in the pillared dark,"

An old creature in a huge, clumsy overcoat,
Lifting his great boots through the drifts,
Going as if to die among "those dark trees"
Of his own country. I watched him go,

Past a house, quiet, warm and light,
A farm, a countryside, a woodpile in its slow
Smokeless burning, alder swamps ghastly white,
Tumultuous snows, blanker whitenesses,
Into the pathless wood, one eye weeping,
The dark trees, for which no saying is dark enough,
Which mask the gloom and lead on into it,
The bare, the withered, the deserted.

There were no more cottages.
Soft bombs of dust falling from the boughs,
The sun shining no warmer than the moon,
He had outwalked the farthest city light,
And there, clinging to the perfect trees,
A last leaf. What was it?
What was that whiteness? — white, uncertain —
The night too dark to know.

4

He turned. *Love,*
Love of things, duty, he said,
And made his way back to the shelter
No longer sheltering him, the house
Where everything real was turning to words,

Where he would think on the white wave,
Folded back, that rides in place on the obscure
Pouring of this life to the sea —
And invent on the broken lips of darkness
The seal of form and the *mot juste.*

5

Poet of the country of white houses,
Of clearings going out to the dark wall of woods
Frayed along the skyline, you who nearly foreknew
The next lines of poems you suddenly dropped,
Who dwelt in access to that which other men
Have burnt all their lives to get near, who heard
The high wind, in gusts, seething
From far off, headed through the trees exactly
To this place where it must happen, who spent
Your life on the point of giving away your heart
To the dark trees, the dissolving woods,
Into which you go at last, heart in hand, deep in:
When we think of a man who was cursed
Neither with the mystical all-lovingness of Walt Whitman
Nor with Melville's anguish to know and to suffer,
And yet cursed . . . A man, what shall I say,
Vain, not fully convinced he was dying, whose calling
Was to set up in the wilderness of his country,
At whatever cost, a man, who would be his own man,
We think of you. And from the same doorway
At which you lived, between the house and the woods,
We see your old footprints going away across
The great Republic, Frost, up memorized slopes,
Down hills floating by heart on the bulldozed land.

PART II

TILLAMOOK JOURNAL (2nd version)

1

I have come here
From Chicago, packing
A sleeping bag, a pan
To melt snow for drinking,
Dried apricots, tea,
And a great boiled beef-
Heart for gnawing on.

Two loggers drove me
As far in as they could get,
Two of the gunnysack loggers
Of the Burn, owning a truck
And a dozer, a few cables
And saws, who drag out
The sound heartwood for money.

They turned around
Where a rockslide had dumped itself,
One of them got out
And reached in the erosion
And showed me a handful
Of earth, more black
Ashes than it was earth.

2

A few years back,
They said, there'd

Been a prospector here,
An old man past seventy
Who believed the land,
Being otherwise worthless,
Ought to yield precious metal.

They would run across him,
A little, swaying heap of gear
Traipsing across
A logging road, or thrashing up
Some avalanching gravel, or
Mumbling about metal while staggering
Out of a vegetable gulley.

A full year
He hunted uranium or gold,
The Geiger counter lashed on
Like an extra heart,
Around January he'd have
Settled for anything at all,
When spring came he vanished.

3

I set out walking
From where they turned,
Underfoot the terrain spews
Loose rock and gravel,
Every step rattles and gives way,
Gigantic treetrunks
Barricade all the directions.

I wondered that a man
Of seventy-odd years had been able
To put up with one of them
On this breast, the ear

Pressed to the metal heart hearing
Only his own bloodbeat
And that getting fainter.

As the hill grew steep,
Up to my ankles in gravel
And grappling at roots and rocks
I traversed and wound along,
At last I came climbing up
On my hands and knees
As though I'd come here begging.

4

From the top of Cedar Butte
The whole compass is visible,
To the west the Pacific
Lies out flat and shiny,
Everywhere else are
Nothing but hills
Plunging across a saw-toothed country.

I looked back south
Where the hills have been logged off,
Except for a few clumps of snags
Out of reach
Or too burnt
Or decayed for profit
It is a total shambles,

White stumps,
White logs washing
To the valleys, bleeding scarps,
Lopped spurs, empty streambeds,
The whole land split and cracked
Under the crisscross of roads
And oozing down its ravines.

5

It is twenty-five years
Since the first blue-white puff
Kited up the wind,
The Douglas fir is an intolerant tree
Potent only in fits,
And breeds best in the open,
As in the aftermath of fire,

Convicts have put saplings
By the coast, schoolboys
Have planted by the highway,
Rain and sun continue falling,
Nothing catches,
A little fireweed, vine maple, grape,
Ants, black spiders . . .

To the north
On hills the loggers can't reach
The great virgin stands
Of snags
Burnt clean and bleached
In the distance keep on
Blurring into smoke.

6

All day the big,
Immaculate snowflakes
Have been coming down, melting
On touching. All night,
Wet through, trying for sleep,
I had to hear Kilchis
River grinding its rocks and boulders.

The ravine is a mass
Of slash slippery
With rain and snow. Uprooted

Trees cross and lock each other
Blocking the water,
Tan, beautifully
Grained rims for the waterfalls.

At last a little
Mule deer joined me,
Leading like a scout,
When I turned off and climbed
He stopped too, and sadly,
It almost seemed, watched my going.
Some birds began wrangling and chirping.

7

At the sound of surf
I scramble to my feet
And climb again — from where I sat
Under the last knoll,
Gnawing the heart,
Looking back at the Burn
As it went out in the twilight,

Its crags broken,
Its valleys soaked in night,
Just one more of the
Plundered breasts of the world —
And hearing my heart
Beat in the air
I come over the last summit

Into a dark wind
Blasting out of the darkness,
Where before me the tempestuous ocean
Falls with long triple crashes on the shore
And where behind the snow is putting down
A last, saprophytic blossoming.
It is only steps to the unburnable sea.

ON HARDSCRABBLE MOUNTAIN

1

On old slashed spruce boughs
Buoying me up off the snow
I stretched out on the mountain,
Now and then a bit of snow
Would slide quietly from a branch,

Once a last deerfly came by,

I could see off for about a hundred miles.

2

I waked with a start,
The sun had crawled off me,
I was shivering in thick blue shadows,
Sap had stuck me to the spruce boughs,

Far away I could hear
The wind again starting to rise.

3

On the way down, passing
The little graveyard in the woods,
I gave a thought to the old skulls and bones lying there,

And I started praying to a bear just shutting his eyes,
To a skunk dozing off,

To a marmot with yellow belly,
To a dog-faced hedgehog,
To a dormouse with a paunch and large ears like leaves or
   wings.

ON FROZEN FIELDS

1

We walk across the snow,
The stars can be faint,
The moon can be eating itself out,
There can be meteors flaring to death on earth,
The Northern Lights can be blooming and seething
And tearing themselves apart all night,
We walk arm in arm, and we are happy.

2

You in whose ultimate madness we live,
You flinging yourself out into the emptiness,
You — like us — great an instant,

O only universe we know, forgive us.

IN FIELDS OF SUMMER

The sun rises,
The goldenrod blooms,
I drift in fields of summer,
My life is adrift in my body,
It shines in my heart and hands, in my teeth,
It shines up at the old crane
Who holds out his drainpipe of a neck
And creaks along in the blue,

And the goldenrod shines with its life, too,
And the grass, look,
The great field wavers and flakes,
The rumble of bumblebees keeps deepening,
A phoebe flutters up,
A lark bursts up all dew.

A BIRD COMES BACK

1

Only the head and shoulders, only
The bust of a bird really,
Cochineal and emerald, appears
Stinging the blossoms, there
At the open window, amidst phlox,
Where there are, already,
Bees and three white butterflies,
His missing wings crackling deeply
As he needles the flowers.

2

The old timbers of the house
Shift sidewise, like stove grates,
One of the too-frequent settlings . . .
I think of Emily Dickinson's hummingbird . . .

3

Odd to see him now
With nothing in back of him
But New Hampshire fifty miles away and badly faded.

CELLS BREATHE IN THE EMPTINESS

1

When the flowers turn to husks
And the great trees suddenly die
And rocks and old weasel bones lose
The little life they suddenly had
And the air quells and goes so still
It gives the ears something like the bends,
It is an eerie thing to keep vigil,
The senses racing in the emptiness.

2

From the compost heap
Now arises the sound of the teeth
Of one of those sloppy green cabbageworms
Eating his route through a cabbage,
Now snarling like a petite chainsaw, now droning on . . .

A butterfly blooms on a buttercup,
From the junkpile flames up a junco.

3

How many plants are really very quiet animals?
How many inert molecules are ready to break into life?

POEMS OF NIGHT

1

I touch your face,
I move my hand over
Slopes, falls, lumps of sight,
Lashes barely able to be touched,
Lips that give way so easily
It's a shock to feel underneath
The hard grin of the bones.

Muffled a little, barely cloaked,
Zygoma, maxillary, turbinate.

2

I put my hand
On the side of your face,
You lean your head a little
Into my hand — and so,
I know you're a dormouse
Taken up in winter sleep,
A lonely, stunned weight
Shut in the natural mystery.

3

A cheekbone,
A curved piece of brow,
A pale eyelid

Float in the dark,
And now I make out
An eye, dark,
Wormed with far-off, unaccountable lights.

4

Hardly touching, I hold
What I can only think of
As some deepest of memories in my arms,
Not mine, but as if the life in me
Were slowly remembering what it is.

You lie here now in your physicalness,
This beautiful degree of reality.

5

And now the day, raft that breaks up, comes on.

I think of a few bones
Floating on a river at night,
The starlight blowing in place on the water,
The river leaning like a wave towards the emptiness.

NIGHTFALL OF THE REAL

I. *House on the Cliff*

Swallows dart at one another
Across the thin curve of the moon. Two
Ravens tumble at the cliff and fall away. On the port
The orange, white, and blue umbrellas
Which have turned all day like sunflowers
Fold themselves. In the Bar des Guitares
They are raking the strings. It is evening.
Mullets are leaping in the straits.

II. *La Nappe Frugale*

On a table set by heart
In the last sun of the day
Olives, three fishes,
Bread, a bottle of rosé.

A rainbow crosses a fish,
A glass blossoms and reblossoms,
Flesh slides off bones which were,
We now see, only stabbing it.

Darkness sticks itself
To empty spines. Night climbs
In glasses. A breeze. Low
Voices. Paths floating on earth.

III. *Hour of the Lamp*

1

Olives, bread,
Fishes, pink wine:
Sudden in the dusk a
Crackling across stones.

To this table one came,
Came and ate, tore actual bread,
Felt physical drink touch his soul,
Here gabbed, here laughed a last time.

2

Four faces looking in
On a vanished room — the vineyard,
The olive grove, the stones,
The green sea — begin vanishing.
In a room ready to turn white

A pause: out in the dark
The distant dull splash of a fish.
Yet again. Sick of weight
It leans up through its eerie life
Towards the night-flash of its emblemhood.

3

All things jump to their shapes.
The spoon, the table, the mirrors,
The green portrait of a vase of flowers,
Each now streaked fatally with dusk.

The generating light goes out,
The rich time, which is twilight,
On this shore in the darkness lies
A fern, fishy, and all but glittering.

MIDDLE OF THE WAY

for Inés

1. I wake in the night,
    An old ache in the shoulder blades.
    I lie amazed under the trees
    That creak a little in the dark,
    The giant trees of the world.

    I lie on earth the way
    Flames lie in the woodpile,
    Or as an imprint, in sperm, of what is to be.
    I love the earth, and always
    In its darknesses I am a stranger.

2. 6 A.M. Water frozen again. Melted it and made tea. Ate
    a raw egg and the last orange. Refreshed by a long sleep.
    The trail practically indistinguishable under 8″ of snow.
    9:30 A.M. Snow up to my knees in places. Sweat begins
    freezing under my shirt when I stop to rest. The woods are
    filled, anyway, with the windy noise of the first streams.
    10:30 A.M. The sun at last. The snow starts to melt off the
    boughs at once, falling with little ticking sounds. Mist
    clouds are lying in the valleys. 11:45 A.M. Slow, glittering
    breakers roll in on the beaches ten miles away, very blue
    and calm, as if it were Honolulu down there. Odd to see
    it while sitting in snow. 12 noon. An inexplicable sense of
    joy, as if some happy news had been transmitted to me di-
    rectly, by-passing the brain. 2 P.M. From the top of Gauldy
    I look back into Hebo valley. Castle Rock sticks into a

cloud. A cool breeze comes up from the valley, it is a fresh, earthly wind and tastes of snow and trees. It is not like those transcendental breezes that make the heart ache. It brings happiness. 2:30 P.M. Lost the trail. A big woodpecker watches me wade about through the snow trying to locate it. The sun has gone back of the trees. 3:10 P.M. Still hunting for the trail. Getting cold. From an elevation I have an open view to the SE, a world of timberless, white hills, rolling, weirdly wrinkled. Above them a pale half moon. 3:45 P.M. Going on by map and compass. I saw a deer a minute ago, he fled touching down every fifteen feet or so. 7:30 P.M. Made camp near the head of Alder Creek. Trampled a bed into the snow and filled it with boughs. Concocted a little fire in the darkness. Ate pork and beans. A slug or two of whisky burnt my throat. The night very clear. Very cold. That half moon is up there and a lot of stars have come out among the treetops. The fire has fallen to coals.

3. The coals go out,
   The last smoke weaves up
   Losing itself in the stars.
   This is my first night to lie
   In the uncreating dark.

   In the heart of a man
   There sleeps a green worm
   That has spun the heart about itself,
   And that shall dream itself black wings
   One day to break free into the beautiful black sky.

   I leave my eyes open,
   I lie here and forget our life,
   All I see is we float out
   Into the emptiness, among the great stars,
   On this little vessel without lights.

I know that I love the day,
The sun on the mountain, the Pacific
Shiny and accomplishing itself in breakers,
But I know I live half alive in the world,
I know half my life belongs to the wild darkness.

RUINS UNDER THE STARS

1

All day under acrobat
Swallows I have sat, beside ruins
Of a plank house sunk to its windows
In burdock and raspberry canes,
The roof dropped, the foundation broken in,
Nothing left perfect but axe-marks on the beams.

A paper in a cupboard talks about "Mugwumps,"
In a V-letter a farmboy in the Marines has "tasted battle . . ."
The apples are pure acid on the tangle of boughs,
The pasture has gone to popple and bush.
Here on this perch of ruins
I listen for the crunch of the porcupines.

2

Overhead the skull-hill rises
Crossed on top by the stunted apple,
Infinitely beyond it, older than love or guilt,
Lie the stars ready to jump and sprinkle out of space.

Every night under the millions of stars
An owl dies or a snake sloughs his skin,
But what if a man feels the dark
Homesickness for the inconceivable realm?

47

3

Sometimes I see them,
The south-going Canada geese,
At evening, coming down
In pink light, over the pond, in great,
Loose, always dissolving V's —
I go out into the field,
Amazed and moved, and listen
To the cold, lonely yelping
Of those tranced bodies in the sky,
Until I feel on the point
Of breaking to a sacred, bloodier speech.

4

This morning I watched
Milton Norway's sky-blue Ford
Dragging its ass down the dirt road
On the other side of the valley.

Later, off in the woods I heard
A chainsaw agonizing across the top of some stump.
A while ago the tracks of a little, snowy,
SAC bomber went crawling across heaven.

What of that little hairstreak
That was flopping and batting about
Deep in the goldenrod —
Did she not know, either, where she was going?

5

Just now I had a funny sensation,
As if some angel, or winged star,

Had been perched nearby watching, maybe speaking.
I turned, in the chokecherry bush
There was a twig just ceasing to tremble . . .

The bats come spelling the swallows.
In the smoking heap of old antiques
The porcupine-crackle starts up again,
The bone-saw, the pure music of this sphere,
And up there the old stars rustling and whispering.

TREE FROM ANDALUSIA

1

This old bleached tree
Dumped on the Sagaponack beach . . .
The wind has lifted and only seethes
Far up among the invisible stars,
Yet I hear in the limbs a tragic voice,
As once on Ferry Street, at night,
Among *to let* signs and closed wholesalers,
From some loft I heard a phrase of jazz,
y recuerdo una brisa triste por los olivos.

2

The wind starts fluting
In our teeth, in our ears,
It whines down the harmonica
Of the fingerbones, moans at the skull . . .

Blown on by their death
The things on earth whistle and cry out.
Nothing can keep still. Only the wind.

SPINDRIFT

1

On this tree thrown up
From the sea, its tangle of roots
Letting the wind go through, I sit
Looking down the beach: old
Horseshoe crabs, broken skates,
Sand dollars, sea horses, as though
Only primeval creatures get destroyed,
At chunks of sea-mud still quivering,
At the light as it glints off the water
And the billion facets of the sand,
At the soft, mystical shine the wind
Blows over the dunes as they creep.

2

Sit down
By the clanking shore
Of this bitter, beloved sea,

Pluck sacred
Shells from the icy surf,
Fans of gold light, sunbursts,

Lift one to the sun
As a sign you accept to go,
As bid, to the shrine of the dead,

And as it blazes
See the lost life within
Alive again in the fate-shine.

3

This little bleached root
Drifted from some foreign shore,
Brittle, cold, practically weightless,

If anything is dead, it is,
This castout worn
To the lost grip it always essentially was.

If it has lost hold
It at least keeps the wild
Shape of what it held,

And it remains the hand
Of that gravel, one of the earth's
Wandering icons of "to have."

4

I sit listening
To the surf as it falls,
The power and inexhaustible freshness of the sea,
The suck and inner boom
As a wave tears free and crashes back
In overlapping thunders going away down the beach.

It is the most we know of time,
And it is our undermusic of eternity.

5

I think of how I
Sat by a dying woman,

Her shell of a hand,
Wet and cold in both of mine,
Light, nearly out, existing as smoke,
I sat in the glow of her wan, absorbed smile.

6

Under the high wind
That moans in the grass
And whistles through crabs' claws
I sit holding this little lamp,
This icy fan of the sun.

Across gull tracks
And wind ripples in the sand
The wind seethes. My footprints
Slogging for the absolute
Already begin vanishing.

7

What does he really love,
That old man,
His wrinkled eyes
Tortured by smoke,
Walking in the ungodly
Rasp and cackle of old flesh?

The swan dips her head
And peers at the mystic
In-life of the sea,
The gull drifts up
And eddies towards heaven,
The breeze in his arms . . .

Nobody likes to die
But an old man
Can know
A kind of gratefulness
Towards time that kills him,
Everything he loved was made of it.

In the end
What is he but the scallop shell
Shining with time like any pilgrim?

FLOWER HERDING
ON MOUNT MONADNOCK

1

I can support it no longer.
Laughing ruefully at myself
For all I claim to have suffered
I get up. Damned nightmarer!

It is New Hampshire out there,
It is nearly the dawn.
The song of the whippoorwill stops
And the dimension of depth seizes everything.

2

The song of a peabody bird goes overhead
Like a needle pushed five times through the air,
It enters the leaves, and comes out little changed.

The air is so still
That as they go off through the trees
The love songs of birds do not get any fainter.

3

The last memory I have
Is of a flower which cannot be touched,

Through the bloom of which, all day,
Fly crazed, missing bees.

4

As I climb sweat gets up my nostrils,
For an instant I think I am at the sea,

One summer off Cap Ferrat we watched a black seagull
Straining for the dawn, we stood in the surf,

Grasshoppers splash up where I step,
The mountain laurel crashes at my thighs.

5

There is something joyous in the elegies
Of birds. They seem
Caught up in a formal delight,
Though the mourning dove whistles of despair.

But at last in the thousand elegies
The dead rise in our hearts,
On the brink of our happiness we stop
Like someone on a drunk starting to weep.

6

I kneel at a pool,
I look through my face
At the bacteria I think
I see crawling through the moss.

My face sees me,
The water stirs, the face,
Looking preoccupied,
Gets knocked from its bones.

7

I weighed eleven pounds
At birth, having stayed on

Two extra weeks in the womb.
Tempted by room and fresh air
I came out big as a policeman
Blue-faced, with narrow red eyes.
It was eight days before the doctor
Would scare my mother with me.

Turning and craning in the vines
I can make out through the leaves
The old, shimmering nothingness, the sky.

8

Green, scaly moosewoods ascend,
Tenants of the shaken paradise,

At every wind last night's rain
Comes splattering from the leaves,

It drops in flurries and lies there,
The footsteps of some running start.

9

From a rock
A waterfall
A single trickle like a strand of wire
Breaks into beads halfway down.

I know
The birds fly off
But the hug of the earth wraps
With moss their graves and the giant boulders.

In the forest I discover a flower.

The invisible life of the thing
Goes up in flames that are invisible
Like cellophane burning in the sunlight.

It burns up. Its drift is to be nothing.

In its covertness it has a way
Of uttering itself in place of itself,
Its blossoms claim to float in the Empyrean,

A wrathful presence on the blur of the ground.

The appeal to heaven breaks off.
The petals begin to fall, in self-forgiveness.
It is a flower. On this mountainside it is dying.